ENCAUSTIC ART

CONTENTS

Cover: Hesseling Design, Ede
Photography: Studio Wim Burgsteijn, Ede
Typesetting and lay-out: Imago desktop publishing, Amersfoort

ISBN 90 384 08366
NUGI 440

Embroidery: Thanks to Jane Champion and Mary Kinsella.
Rubber stamps used courtesy of personal stamp exchange.

FOREWORD

Encaustic Art is a fascinating hobby that can be developed into an art. If you can't paint you can still be creative but you must be willing to try something new and sometimes to take a little risk. Coloured waxes have been used for artwork for more than 2000 years. There are great advantages in using heat as a solvent instead of slow drying liquid paints like oil or water colour. The basic encaustic techniques are simple and give results that are almost instantly finished. The wax colours may be reworked with heat at any future time so if you want to change something in your work you can!

Electrical tools are easy to control, easy to clean and pleasant to handle. Just plug in, switch on and you can start. If you need to stop just turn off the power and everything freezes until the next time it is turned on!

Over the last few years the author of this book – Michael Bossom – has developed simple methods for learning to use wax and heat to create fascinating and imaginative works. Through the spread of knowledge by his teaching several other companies have now joined in the marketing of these methods with a variety of materials becoming available.

All the techniques in this book relate to the use of Encaustic Art wax blocks and sticks for the art quality colours. The Encaustic Art low heat tools have been used and Encaustic Art painting card for all white card applications. When following the experiments and projects in this book you are advised to use these Encaustic Art materials and tools for best results.

NOTE
The diagrams in this book have been carefully designed to help you produce good results quickly. Following them exactly will speed your learning process.

INTRODUCTION

Encaustic Art is fun. Everyone can create interesting and often fascinating artwork with this easy to start activity.
It can be a hobby, it can be a craft and it can be an art.

Low heat tools are used to melt carefully formulated wax which is coloured with lightfast pigments. These brilliant colours can easily be worked into unlimited patterns. With a little more care the four basic types of effect produced by the painting iron can be put together to form simple landscapes. These simplest ideas are just the beginning.

This book has been written to help you enjoy the satisfaction and fascination you will find when you work with Encaustic Art. It is an ideal activity for every age group from child right through to old age. Even if you have no skill at all you will be surprised by your own results.
For those who paint in other mediums Encaustic Art has some very special qualities to offer. This wax medium is fantastically versatile. Any fine artist will know that encaustic wax has instant workability and will last for thousands of years if crafted with art quality materials.

Hobby is a reflection of your interest and enjoyment.
Craft is the development and use of skills – the practical side of your hobby.
Art is about your awareness – the way you perceive and understand what is all around. Examples are the senses of colour, composition, perspective and form, etc.
All these qualities can be developed and I hope that through the projects, ideas, techniques and comments in these pages you will find a growing enthusiasm to work, to learn and to continue.

Wales 1994

You are as you are.
To be different requires change.
Creativity incites change.
M.B. 1986

A BRIEF HISTORY

Painting with wax is not new. The Ancient Greeks, Romans and Egyptians all used beeswax mixed with earth pigments for painting portraits onto a wood base. The coloured beeswax was often mixed with a resin such as damar or shellac to create a harder and tougher mixture. Encaustic methods were being practised long before oil paints were developed and they have proved to be extremely durable through time.

It is believed that the waxes were heated in containers over a charcoal fire until molten and then applied to the wood with brushes or perhaps heated spatulas. "Soul" or "Burial" portraits were a favourite subject and examples from almost 2,000 years ago can readily be seen in various museums around the world.

Encaustic methods have been used through the ages by a small number of artists and were popular for some types of icon painting. However other media like oils and tempera caused a decline in work with wax colours until more recent times when electrically operated tools have become available. These new low-temperature tools allow control of the wax colours and enable easy working methods. Encaustic Art is back!

Various artists from around the world have used encaustic waxes to create unusual works combining vivid colours and textures, etc. But it is really only in the past few years that the spread of simple methods has stimulated and inspired a much larger cross section of people to experiment with this art.

Now hobbyists, crafts people, artists and even those who believed they could not paint are all finding achievement, interest and satisfaction in the activity and revival of Encaustic Art.

ARTIMEDORUS

MODERN MATERIALS

Waxes

Encaustic Art waxes are specially formulated to provide art quality colour in a safe non-toxic form which is designed to be used when melted. The melting temperature is just over 62°c (140°f). All colours are intermixable. Some pigments are transparent whilst others are opaque. Some are thick in consistency whilst others are more liquid when molten. The waxes have a pleasant natural odour and are easy to work with either when being held or if laid flat on the work surface. These wax blocks and sticks are extremely versatile. The projects and ideas in this book outline a few of the many applications possible.

Many types of wax exist but normal children's crayons are not generally suitable. Other types of wax are offered for encaustic painting but will behave according to their specific formulation and cannot be guaranteed effective for all of the encaustic heat techniques described in this book.

Painting card and other base materials

To enable re-working of the wax it must not be absorbed into the white card surface too quickly. Encaustic Art painting card has been specially impregnated and enables the wax to slide around on the surface without allowing too much absorbtion. The card resists heat damage and is tough and flexible.

Wax can be applied to many types of surface. High gloss coloured card is available in many shades but remember that wax can flake off a high gloss surface. Absorbent card and paper can be used but once applied the painting can't be changed easily. Wood, fabric, plastic, metal, etc. all provide different potentials.

Working materials

Any slightly absorbent paper without heavy printing will work well as a disposable covering for your work surface. Favourites are news print offcuts or computer paper. Tissues are necessary for cleaning the low heat tools. Soft boxed tissue (eg. Kleenex) are ideal and can also be used to carefully polish finished encaustic artwork.

TOOLS FOR ENCAUSTIC ART

"Encaustic" means "to burn in" and this burning refers to heat as the solvent and the way of making the wax liquid and workable. Heated tools are therefore essential to many of the techniques.

The **Encaustic painting iron** is the main tool used in early work. The base plate is used to smooth and texture the wax whilst the edge can scrape and slide through the medium. The tip or point can draw in finer details. It looks rather like a travel iron but displays several important differences.

a. A polished non-coated base for smooth application of the wax and easy cleaning.
b. A very high quality thermostat to allow any temperature required to be set and then ensure that it remains stabe during work.
c. A detachable handle which enables the iron to be turned upside down and used as a small hot plate.

NOTE

- If domestic dry irons are used please expect difficulties in accurate temperature control. Steam irons are not suitable for normal styles of work!

The **Encaustic art stylus** brings the control necessary for finer detail. It operates at a constant low temperature and feels like a thick and very long pen to hold. Interchangeable tips allow different types of work and style to be developed.

The **drawing tip** behaves like a pen nib. Simply touch the heated tip against the wax and a slotted reservoir fills. Then draw lines or colour in areas, etc.

The **brush head** is made from thin copper wires and works like a rigid brush. Be careful not to press too hard or it will bend and may become tangled.

Cold brushes can also be used with liquid wax warmed and held in metal containers similar to the working methods of the Ancients.

Hot air guns and hair dryers bring new possibilities for blowing and running the wax around. These techniques are more advanced but enable some stunning effects to be achieved. Sgraffito techniques are possible with the **Scribing tool**. The pointed and bladed ends offer many possibilities for scraping and scratching waxes off the card.

Encaustic art wax blocks and sticks can also be used cold as crayons.

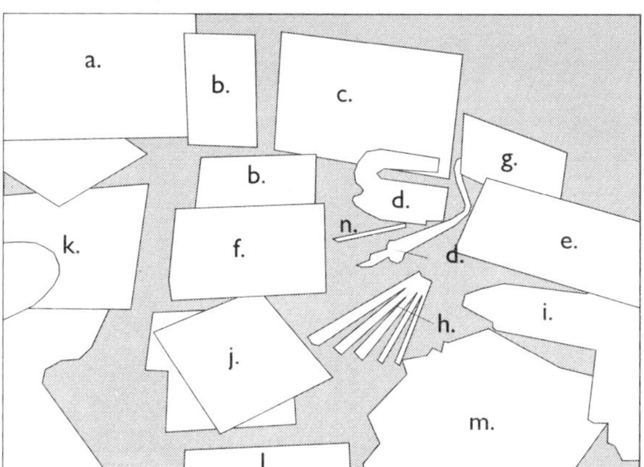

a. Encaustic painting
b. Encaustic art video ①
c. Encaustic art set
d. Painting iron (mint green)
e. Stylus pack
f. Encaustic art mini-set
g. Encaustic art stylus
h. Painting brushes (hair)
i. Example of heat gun
j. Encaustic art waxes
k. Encaustic on fabric
l. Basic instruction book
m. Encaustic painting card
n. Scribing tool (sgraffito)

PREPARING A WORK AREA & TESTING THE IRON TEMPERATURE

Organising your working area carefully will improve the quality of your encaustic artwork! Allow a table area about 36" wide and 18" deep (900mm by 450mm).
A painting board this size could be prepared to save time. This can be brought out when required or quickly and easily stored away when not in use.
Assemble a "pad" of flat newspaper or thick solid card, disposable covering paper (also used as the changeable paper directly under the painting card), tissues, waxes, card, a painting iron and a power supply (ideally with at least 2 socket outlets). Lay out the right handed work area as shown using tape to position the covering paper. If you are left handed mirror the positions of everything.

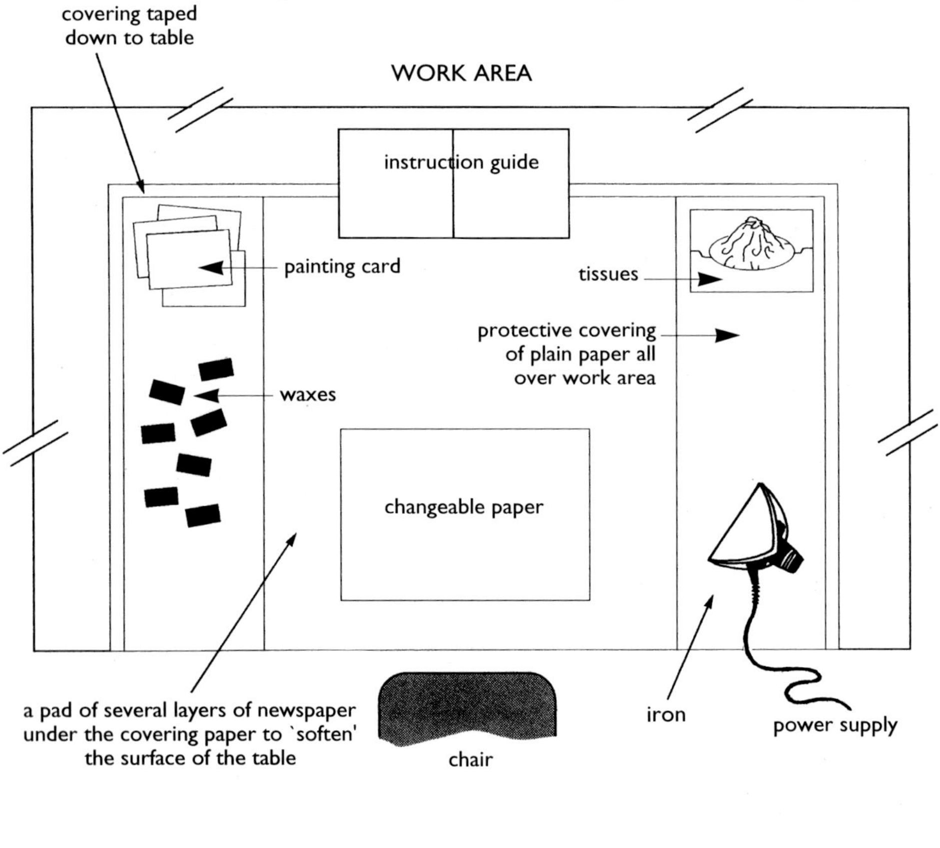

When the work area is ready plug your Encaustic painting iron into the power socket and set the thermostat dial to LOW (similar to NYLON setting 1). Choose a darker wax colour (since these tend to be thicker) and test the iron temperature as shown. If the wax is watery it is too hot so turn down the iron just a little and try again. Better too cool than too hot!

setting the heat of the iron

Loading the iron by melting wax on the horizontal surface

The molten wax should dribble very slowly down the face of the vertical iron
Setting 1 or 'low' temperature

FOUR BASIC TYPES OF EFFECT

There are four basic types of effect that the iron can easily make. Right handed people must load the iron with wax as illustrated on page 11 but left hander's must mirror the process. Always hold the iron in your best hand, and don't be tempted to swap hands when loading the iron with wax. Try the following techniques to get a feel of the four basic effects.

1. Very lightly smooth the wax similar to an ironing motion.

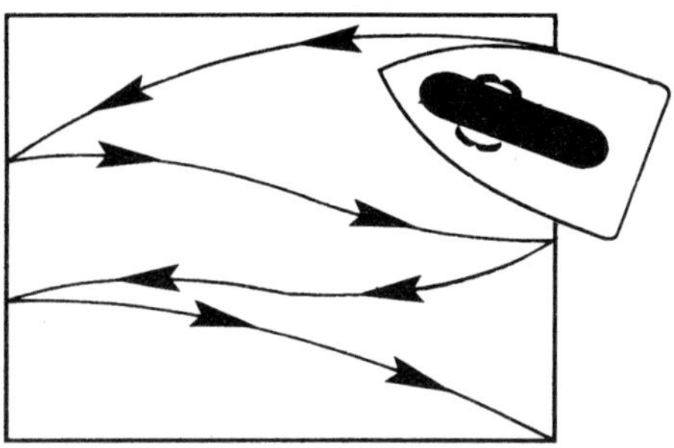

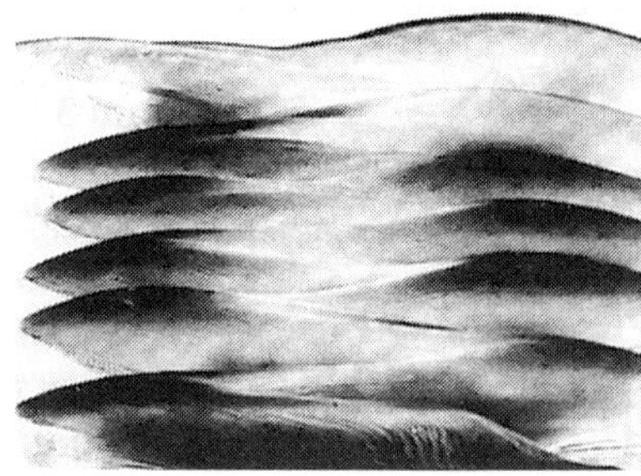

2. Lift the iron off the waxed card quite quickly.

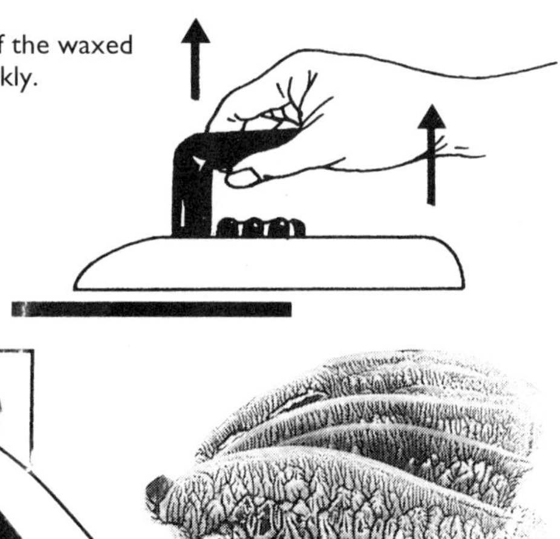

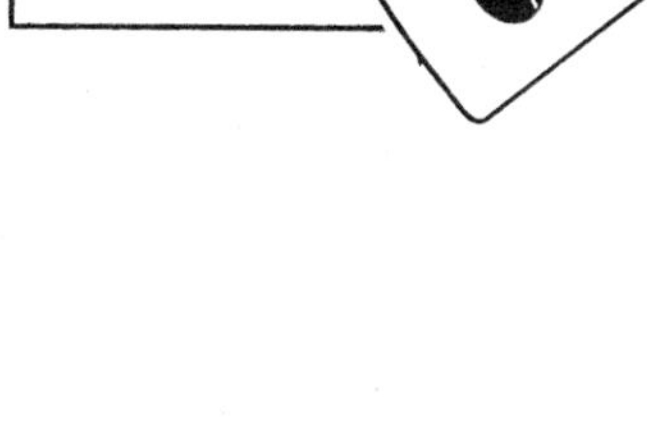

3. Push and slide the iron's edge carefully through the wax.

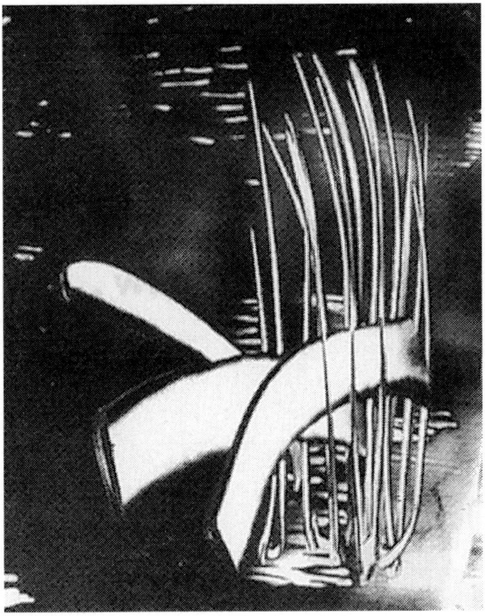

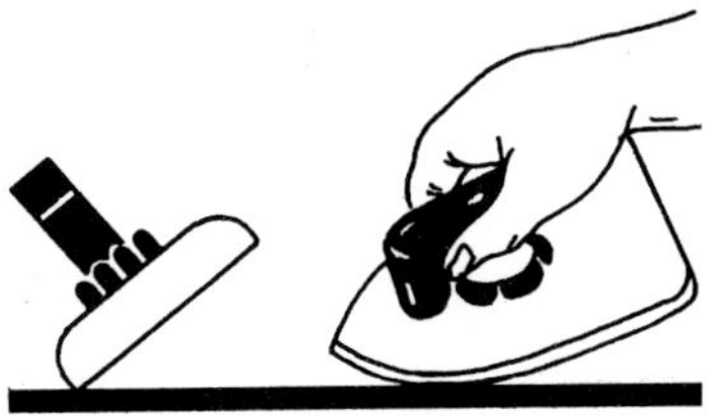

4. Use the iron point dry to scrape thin lines onto the waxed card or lay the wax down on the table and dip the point into it. The heat will melt the wax which can then be applied to waxed or dry card creating small detailed marks.

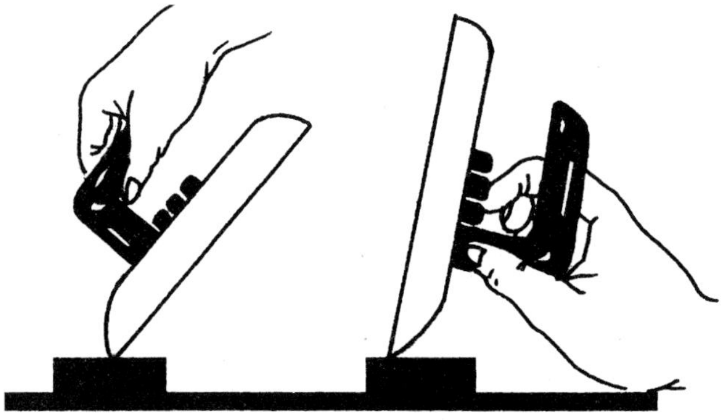

ABSTRACT PATTERNS FOR FUN & CARDS

Abstract designs and fascinating patterns are simple and exciting to make with Encaustic Art. Start with just one or two colours because too many together will quickly become over mixed. Explore different colour combinations and learn a little about colour harmony. Remember that Encaustic Art encourages your creativity and that means you have to try different ideas and explore. You must take risks!

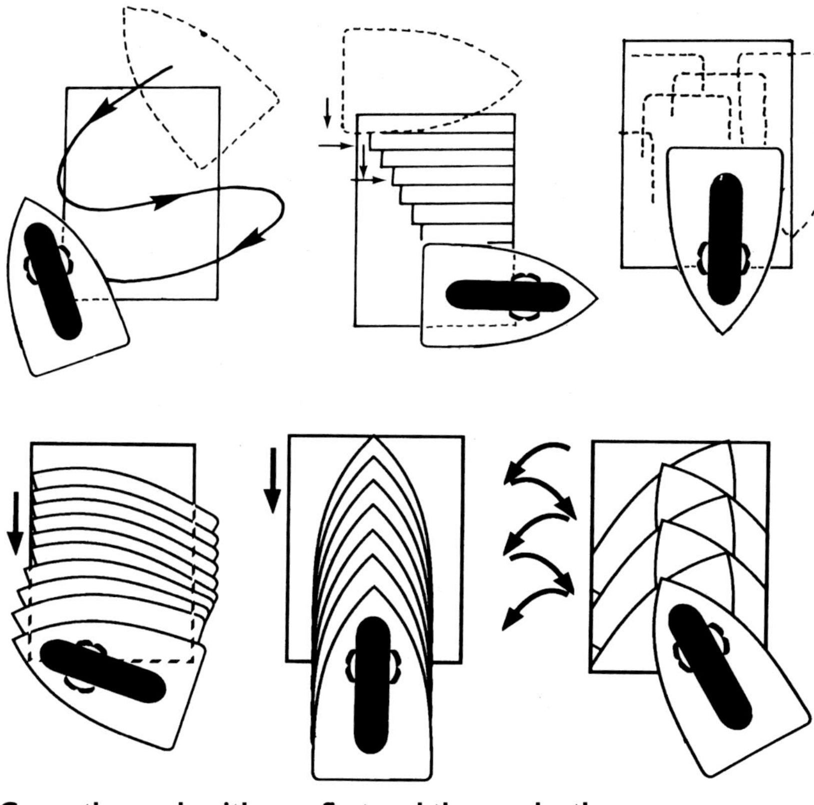

Cover the cards with wax first and then make the creative patterns.

MAKING CARDS, BOOKMARKS & TAGS

Abstract designs can be used as whole paintings or cut into smaller pieces if desired. To finish the surface of the wax image fold a piece of soft boxed tissue into a pad and very lightly polish the whole surface. These artworks can fulfil many decorative uses. Numerous passpartout and aperture cards are commercially available. They come in different sizes with different cut out shapes, colours and borders (see page 14). Alternatively make your own from folded card and stick your designs on the front.
Although no further finishing is necessary there are occasions when the wax needs to be protected against being scratched. Also remember the wax will remelt above 62°c (140°f).

Protection against scratching

1. **Spray fixative** - Fast drying spray varnish in either gloss or matt works well. Spray light even coats over the artwork until all the wax surface is covered. Hair lacquer will work (try the ones you have), but for your best artwork use a commercial art quality product (eg Sprayfix made by 3M).

2. **Clear adhesive film** - the type used to cover books, can be applied direct to the wax image. This is ideal for items like bookmarks, or anything that will be handled often. Cut the clear film large enough to enable generous flaps to fold round and stick to the back of the card.

LANDSCAPE FROM FOUR EFFECTS

Following the diagram instructions below should produce a picture similar to the painting on page 18. Practise this compilation of the four iron effects. Working confidently will give better results than overworking and fiddling. Try this image with the blue green wax first then practise and experiment with other colours.

1 Set iron to '1' or 'low'.

Load the iron as shown with plenty of wax, then spread the wax onto the card but don't press down hard. Slide the iron very lightly!
Put waxed iron on card and spread across.

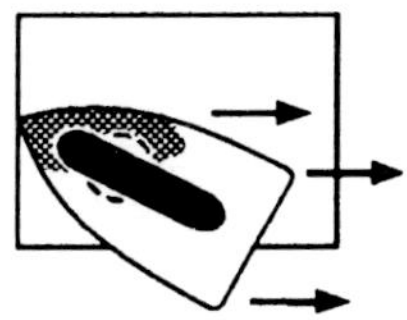

2 Place iron on lower half of wax. Lift like

a hinged lid of a box...
Hold the top of the card down with your free hand and lift the iron off with a quick movement.

3 Put iron on edge. Slide iron on edge

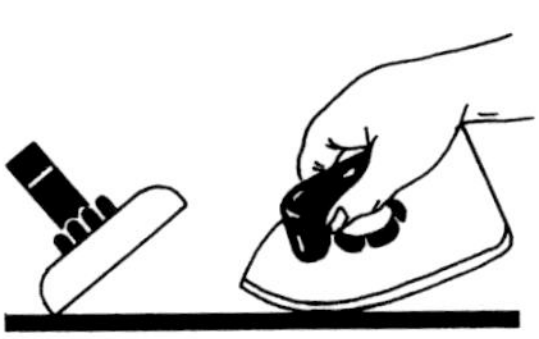

upwards through wax, onto clean area.
Use the rounded edge of the iron and push gently forward like an ice skate cutting through ice. Don't

4 Use point to put in some details.
Hold iron as is easiest. Touch tip into wax block quickly. Don't put too much wax onto the tip of the iron. Re-load if necessary.

Practice this simples landscape on small pieces of the card until yo start to become familiar with the effects. Working quickly and boldly is better than fiddling about. Lightly polish the finished work when it is cool using a soft tissue pad.

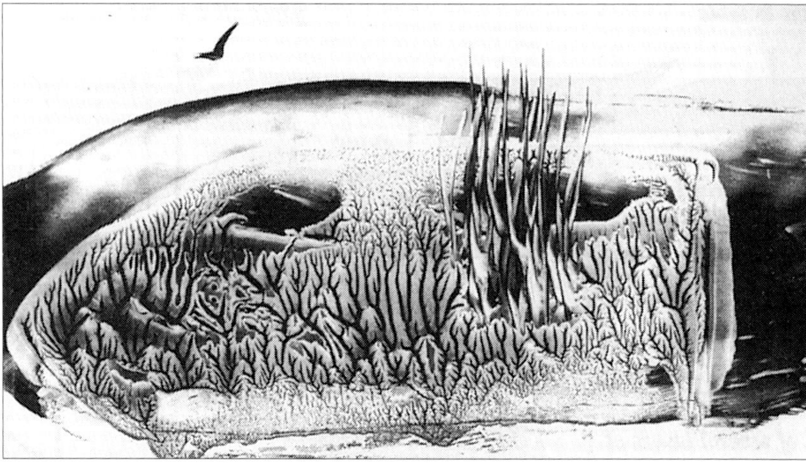

WHAT IS LANDSCAPE?

When you paint from your imagination there is no "right" or "wrong" since you are not trying to imitate and represent something you see. We are surrounded by landscape, so that is the subject easiest to use for learning about the basic concepts involved in painting. No painting will ever become a landscape. It can only ever be a painting and is actually an illusion of a landscape. It may be a good or bad illusion. We are going to start learning with a very simple and easy one. This landscape can be divided into 3 bands of effect. These are sky which is light, distance which will be a medium colour remaining indistinct and finally a foreground containing stronger colours with sharper distinct details.

light

medium, distant
less distinct

stronger colour,
more detailed
and definite

IS IT LANDSCAPE OR SEASCAPE?

This project will exercise the skills covered so far and also show how the same picture painted in different colours can cause quite different interpretations of the image. First follow the instructions using green and white to create the landscape version. Then try another card but use blue and white for seascape. Remember to use clean disposable underpaper when you change from green to blue and try to keep the iron strokes parallel across the card.

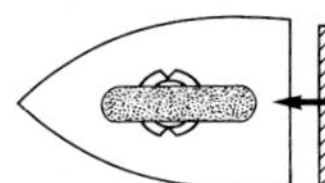
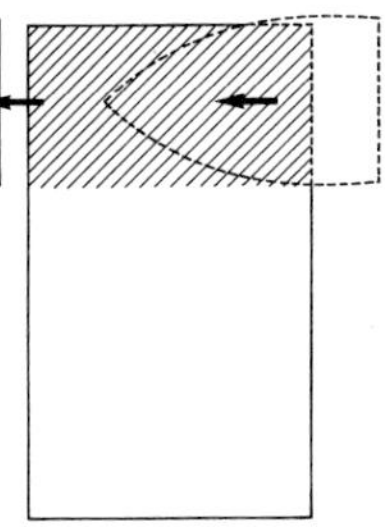

Melt wax on this part of the iron for each new section

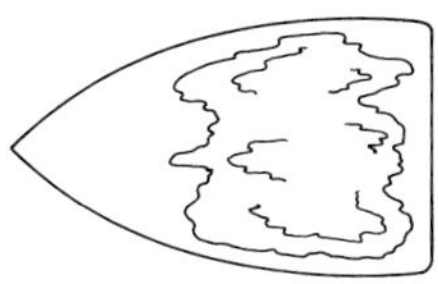

Use light wax - white with a touch of colour

Use more colour this time

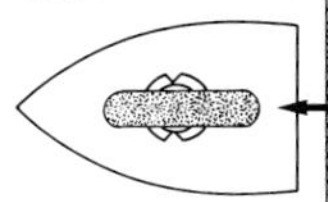

Use the strongest colour for the last section

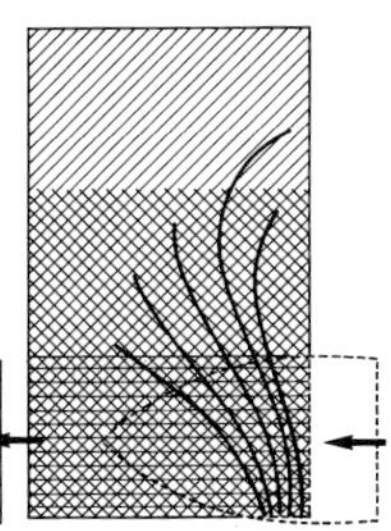
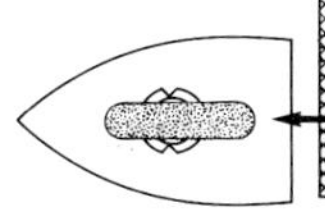

Finally add some detail. Lift off for texture in dark foreground then make 'grasses' by sliding the edge.

A COMPLETE IRON PAINTED LANDSCAPE

Sky - The quality of light in the sky affects the whole feel of the picture. Dull light gives a dull picture whilst warm light gives a warm picture. Try to keep your colours light and clean to obtain fresh looking results. Place clean paper under your card before attempting the sky area. Clean the iron by melting on clear wax and wipe with tissues until no more dirt comes off. Take extra care around the edges and especially along the bottom groove (wax collects here!).

Follow the diagrams carefully and be sure to use plenty of white wax with just a little colour. Create this sky by turning the card around so that when you apply the wax the iron can be pulled towards you. This movement gives smoother action and easier skies. Float the iron lightly over the card in one complete pass. Start with just a little blue in the white. Practise on further cards by using slightly more colours, maybe adding some pink or yellow to the initial mix of waxes. If the colours are too dark re apply light colours over the top.

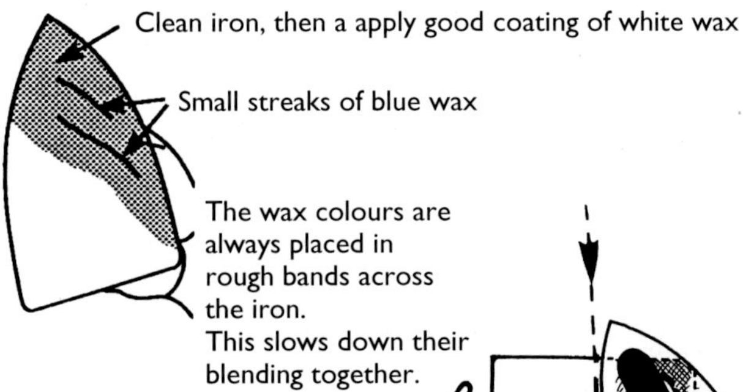

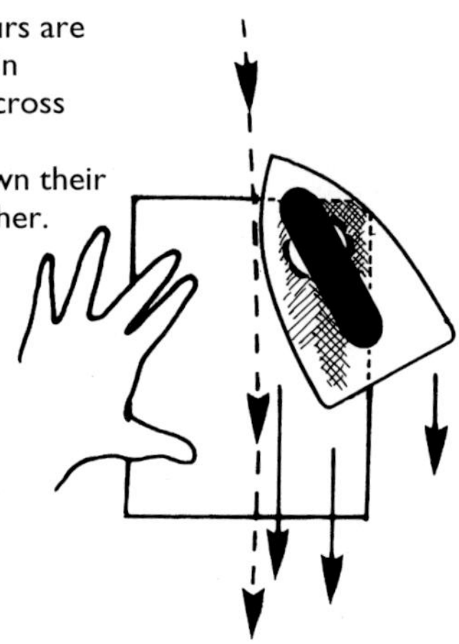

Drag the iron down the card lightly. Try to keep the wax on the card. If it mixes up too much put some more light colours on.

Landscape - To create a more realistic hillscape use the Zig-Zag technique. Load the iron as shown with dark green and light brown wax. Use plenty of wax and do not press too hard or results may be disappointing. Use cards without sky to practise first.

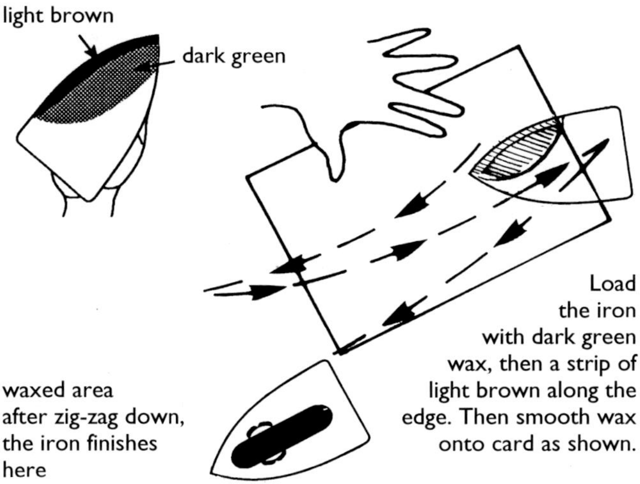

If the iron sticks lift it off then gently replace it and do not press hard. If the card is not fully covered smooth further over the edges as shown in the diagram. Be careful on the return stroke of the iron not to rub out the effects you have just made!
When you are confident enough put this zig-zag landscape under a sky by slightly overlapping the sky area.

BETTER FOREGROUND & PERSPECTIVE

The foreground effect is caused by suction between the card and the iron. When the iron is lifted off the card air rushes into the space and forms the channel patterns that resemble foliage. Working on a rigid surface forces the iron's edge to touch the card and leave "arc marks" behind. These do not look natural so it is much better to lift and bend the card using a **dabbing technique** with the iron to achieve more irregular edge effects.

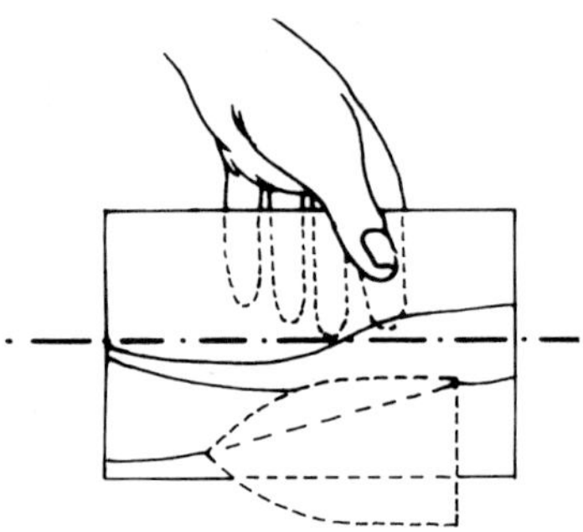

Hold the card lightly with your fingers just above the place you wish to dab. As you work in different areas move your fingers to support the card.

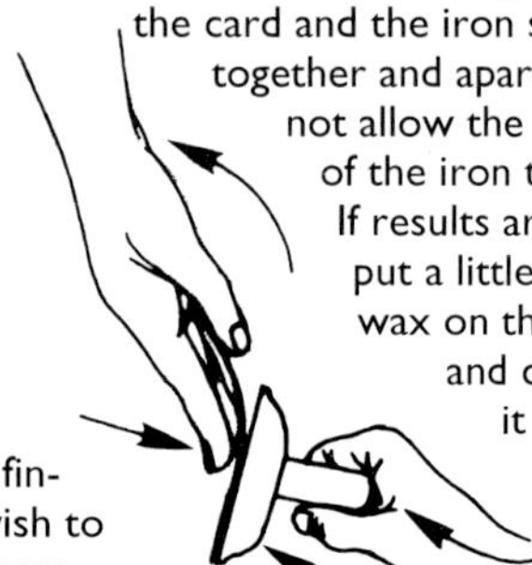

Make contact with the bottom edge of the iron and the card. Lightly spring the card and the iron surface together and apart but do not allow the top edge of the iron to touch. If results are poor put a little more wax on the iron and check that it is not too hot!

ADDING SIMPLE DEPTH & PERSPECTIVE

Now combine the ironed sky with a zig-zag landscape and some dabbing in the foreground. Depth can be improved by adding simplest perspective. In the picture below the grasses provide the "element".
In the foreground add large grasses by sliding the edge of the iron carefully through the wax. To make stronger coloured lines first slide the edge of the iron across the green wax block then apply it to the card. Next try using the tip to add smaller and finer grasses in the upper foreground. The brain now identifies both sets of similar grass shapes as the same thing (grasses) and reasons that the small version must be further away because it is smaller. This creates an illusion of depth. The "element" could be anything repeated in this large/small technique. eg. posts, birds, trees, buildings, figures, etc.

FINER CONTROL USING THE STYLUS

The iron's tip can be used easily for some simple details like birds. But it is difficult to use to draw lines or finer graphic designs. However the **Encaustic art stylus** has been specially developed for this purpose. It operates at a fixed low temperature and enables drawing and brushing techniques to be used.

Drawing tip – has a slot reservoir and operates much like an old style ink pen. Just touch the slotted tip against the block and the heat causes the wax to melt and fill the reservoir channel. Place the drawing tip down with the open slot touching the card and the wax will start to flow. Move with steady confident strokes for smooth lines. Ideal for drawing , writing, colouring in small areas and also colour mixing in small quantities. Clean by wiping in a piece of tissue.

Colour mixing card palette – Using the hot tip mix small amounts of colour together on a card. This colour can be re-used at any future time and with the heated tip of the stylus wax colour is easy to remelt and pick up ready for application. Refer to the central diagram on page 59 for basic colour mixing and colour value (light or dark variation).

The stylus drawing tip is ideal for detail and graphic work.

Heated brush head – is made from copper wires which conduct heat well. The brush head must be used carefully. Do not stab it into the wax block or the wires will bend and tangle. This tool allows colours to be added to your work or mixed within the painting. Excellent for adding or refining small detailed areas, etc. For perfect cleaning melt the brush into some clear wax and then carefully 'pinch' the brush head fibres in a tissue held between your finger and thumb. Pull the tissue away from the stylus tool so that the copper fibres remain straight. Avoid bending or tangling the copper fibres.

Birds, dragonflies, dot flowers, castles...

ADD DETAILS TO YOUR LANDSCAPE

Landscapes containing sky, background and foreground are what can be thought of as "space boxes". Although they only have two dimensions of height and width they also give an illusion of the third dimension - depth. So a "space box" or "place" now exists and can be enhanced with objects to increase descriptive detail and the three dimensional quality.

Colour harmony requires a balance of colour within the image. The easiest way to achieve this is to dab some darker versions of the sky colours into the foreground to create a pleasing blend. With a blue and pink sky for example melt a little dark blue and red violet by scribbling on the iron base then dab them into the foreground foliage. Do not use too much colour. Remember that too much wax can be removed from your card by dabbing the iron then wiping the waxy iron base onto a tissue (laid flat on the table) to clean off the wax. Alternatively to completely remove an area of colour heat the waxed card with a stroke of the iron and use a tissue pad to wipe off the wax whilst it is warm and liquid.

Man made – landscapes tend to display system and uniformity. Trees and flowers planted at equal distances, vertical walls and many straight or uniform lines and shapes.

In contrast **nature** displays an irregular pattern. Nature's system is affected by the environment. The wind encourages trees to lean away form its prevailing direction, poor soil grows smaller plants, seeds are randomly scattered.

Stones – use the tip edge of the iron to scrape away some wax then dab over the area to blend the edges into the foreground.

Birds – collect a spot of wax on the tip of the iron. Place this wax blob on the card. Use tip to flick from the blob, first to the right then again from the blob to the left. Big blobs make big birds!

CHRISTMAS CARDS

Hand made cards are lovely gifts to give and receive. At Christmas everybody makes an effort to contact and greet their friends and family. Encaustic cards are unusual and fascinating for the receiver so try making and sending some – perhaps based on these projects.

Winterlandscape through a window

This interesting card is based on the techniques of landscape covered already and then taken a step further by "framing" the image within a painted window. Follow the diagrams and start by making the landscape. Remember only the central area will actually remain when the card is finished. The rest will become the window and curtains. This card can illustrate any time of year depending on the colours you choose.

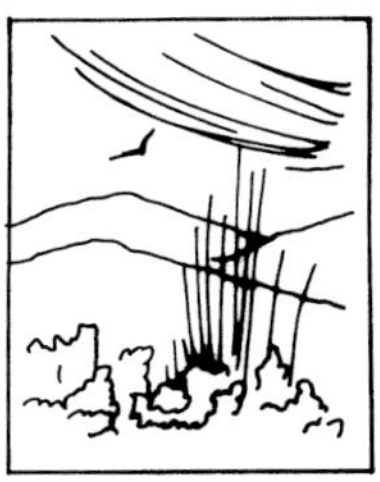

First paint a landscape in winter colours - look outside!

Try to include the shape of horizon from the area where you live.

Now insert:
1. window rails
2. sill
3. top curtains

* use iron with no wax. Whilst card is still warm wipe curtain areas clean, then paint in the colour with the iron.

4. bottom curtains
5. greetings

Mount in a premade card. Remember - you can use a spray coating to protect the image from scratching.

FESTIVE CANDLES

Candles bring a sense of wonder and add a unique atmosphere to special occasions. It is an intriguing touch to use encaustic waxes containing beeswax to represent beeswax candles!
There are a number of ways to create the candles but try just two methods. First using the wax blocks as crayons and second using the stylus brush head which enables rich colour to flood into the candle forms.

Crayon in candles using square edge of wax block or flood in colour with the stylus brush.
Try red or gold to start.
Apply the flame with iron tip or stylus brush or tip.

Dab in the surrounding foliage.
For red candles first use green then dab over again with a little red.

Add scribbled lines of gold or silver 'streamers' over the dabbed borders. Crayon a little yellow colour over the inner foliage area to look like reflected candle light.

MORE CHRISTMAS CARDS

Snowmen, snow and silver bells
Snowmen are festive and fun. The image is held dear in the minds of children. This card incorporates some techniques of work with the **scribbing tool**. This tool is used to scratch and scrape away the wax to reveal the card underneath (sgraffito).

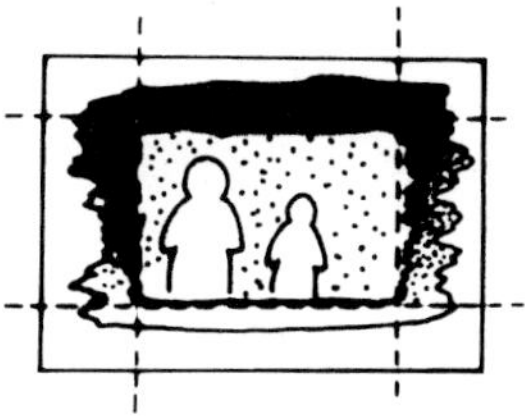

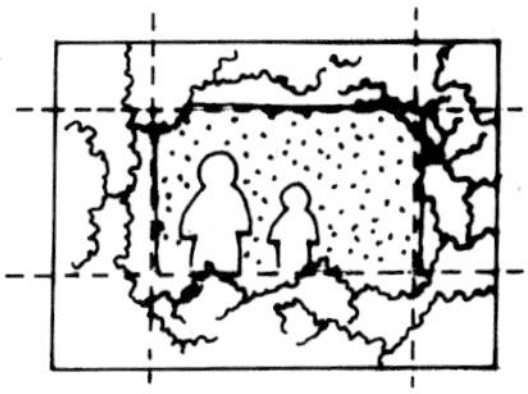

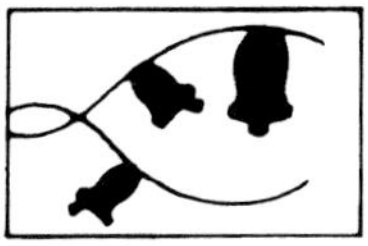

Cover the card with a smooth coating of black blue wax. Clean the iron and rework the bottom half to create some lighter area – the snow!
Use tissue to rub the area clean if necessary.

Next scrape out the snowmen forms using the scribing tool. Scratch in spots and small lines for the snow. Wipe away wax flakes to clean the card. Twist some tissue into a point and rub away any dirt still remaining within the snowmen. Rememeber - only use the central area.

Smooth a frame around the snowman scene with the iron. Dab around the framed area but leave some square frame showing. Try using green and red for a festive feel.

With the stylus tip add details and scarves to the snowmen. Finally use silver wax to decorate the border with streamers and bells.

A CHRISTMAS TREE

Fir trees are remembered by us all at Christmas but they add beauty and character to our landscapes all year round. To draw or paint anything well requires patience, effort and understanding of the subject – that is all. Practise is the key and use of reference material will help (pictures, photos). The **stylus brush head** is the ideal tool for fir trees.

Use the stylus brush with great care. Allow the brush fibres to melt into the wax in their own time. Always keep them straight.

Paint a fir three

Use dark green wax and make a generous straight line slightly to one side of the centre and parallel with the sides. Now fan out the brush fibres carefully and patiently drag out the line of wax into a long triangular shape.

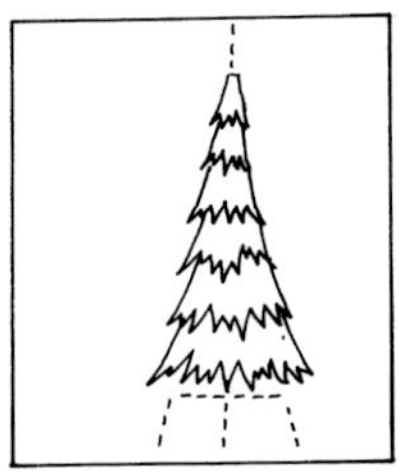

Next apply small quantities of green wax in semi-circular bands across the triangular form working from the top down. Create slightly ragged bottom edges.

Decorate the tree with balls - use the scribing tool to scratch off wax in round shapes, then apply clean colours into these balls. Add the star, a few streamers and parcels, then use the iron to smooth on a narrow border and decorate this with abstract effects.

ENCAUSTIC "APPLIQUE" CARDS

Another approach to seasonal cards is use of "applique" images. These are cut out forms of images associated with a time or event. You will be able to think of images for celebrations from easter to passing your driving test!

The methods are very simple. First paint your card. This could be abstract, landscape or a more definite image like the Christmas cards on the previous pages. Then make a suitable piece of waxed card considering the textures and colours desired. Finally cut out the silhouette shapes you need and stick them either on the painted card or the border. Remember that aperture and passpartout cards are available with many precut internal shapes eg. hearts, windows, etc. Trace these, or other images, or draw your own!

Valentines card (See page 28.)

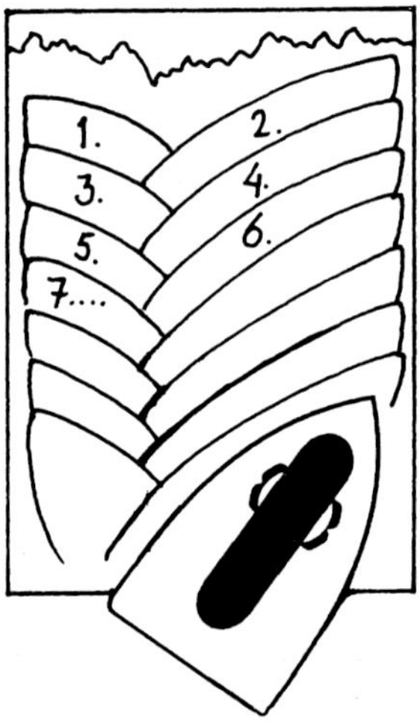

Cover a card with red wax. Use the rounded edge of the iron to create an abstract as shown.

Mount this abstract in a heart shaped cutout card. Remember you can add protection to the wax by spray fixing.
Finally coat a piece of card with red wax, trace the hearts silhouette on page 33, cut it out of the red card and stick it onto the border area.

Easter cards

Put your landscape into a mount to check how it looks.
Decide what silhouette images to use.
Trace them or draw them onto tracing paper.

Apply whatever colour of wax you wish to use onto some painting card. Then cut out the silhouette designs. You may wish to further decorate these with the stylus.

Finally stick the silhouette images to the card and border.

Easter with rabbit & butterflies

PRINTING ON FABRIC

Heat melts wax and this enables wax pictures to be quickly and effectively transferred to fabric. To make a wax print you first make a normal wax painting on card. This is going to be the wax transfer. Try to create a painting with a good even coating of wax but no thick blobs.
When the encaustic transfer has been made choose a piece of white or light coloured natural or absorbent fabric like cotton or silk which has a fine weave. Place clean under-paper on the work area, cover with a piece of tissue (3 tissues thick for silks) and carefully lay your fabric down flat. Then position the transfer where you wish to print it with the waxed side against the fabric. Cover the back of the wax transfer with tissue to keep the fabric clean then iron over the back area of the card (set heat just above low or nylon). As the heat penetrates it remelts the wax which is absorbed into the fabric fibres.

wax transfer method of printing onto fabric.

- Too much wax looks heavy and loses detail whilst too little wax and no transfer of colour is made.
- Non-absorbent fabric can quickly become saturated with wax.
- Coarse weave fabric will give an indistinct print.
- If the iron is too hot some heavy details may blur.
- If the iron is too cold the wax will not melt sufficiently.
- Just about any fabric can be wax printed but when non-absorbent types are hot washed to remove the wax most of the colour will also wash out.

What about washing the fabric?

For clothing items remove the wax by giving one very short hot wash by hand. From then on hand wash in warm water. If the fabric is for embroidery or other decorative purposes it can remain unwashed but may sometimes colour light embroidery thread as you sew. If this seems likely wash the waxed fabric before embroidering.

ENCAUSTIC FOR EMBROIDERY

Wax transfer prints on fabric provide stimulating yet subtle backgrounds for embroidery work and also offer interesting qualities for patchwork, quilting and applique techniques. Pictures or designs are painted onto card in the normal way but it is important not to use too little or too much colour. A generous even coating of wax will give the best print. Start by experimenting with small cards on scrap material. If results are too weak use more wax, if too strong use less. Each waxed card can only successfully be used once for printing. It can be rewaxed and used again. Images on fabric can be built up from several prints so interesting abstracts can evolve or pictures may be blended together.

In embroidery, machine or hand work styles from cross stitch to french knots etc, can be applied. Stitches can be used to strengthen or cover areas. For instance if you want to break up a dark area simply stitch over with light threads. Collage techniques introduce a new and exciting element where all sorts of materials can be brought together. Experiment and enjoy the satisfaction of developing your own styles.

WAX PRINT ON A T-SHIRT OR TIE

Keep your designs simple at the start. Perhaps print an assembly of small pictures on a t-shirt or a small feature area only if working on a tie.

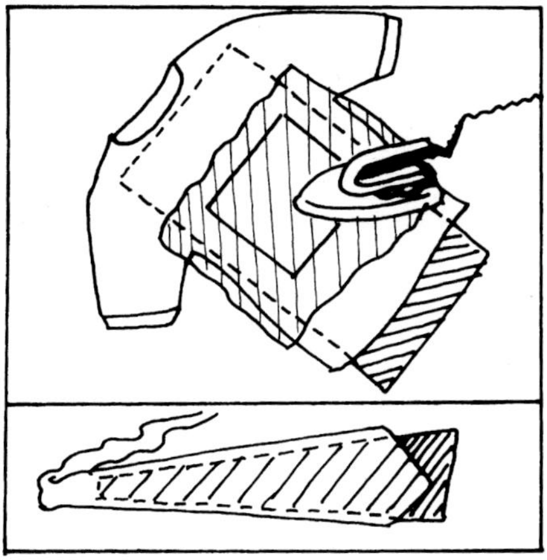

Paint your picture or design onto card. Either leave the edges square, cut them to any shape you wish or tear them for a less formal edge.

Insert a barrier of card under the printing area of the teeshirt or silk tie to stop the wax transmitting to the under fabric. Cut a narrow strip to fit inside a tie. Before inserting lay a tissue on top of the barrier layer. Position the image where you wish to print. Cover with tissue. Turn up the iron's heat midway between low * and high **. Then iron to make the transfer. Look under the card to check the transfer is complete. Then finally seperate card and fabric whilst still warm. For sharp details like birds or grasses use the stylus to draw directly onto the fabric. Colour can also be crayoned on then ironed in using a tissue to protect the fabric.

COVERING BOXES WITH FABRIC

Fabric can be used in numerous ways and for countless applications. It can be made into garments, furnishings or used decoratively as wall hangings, etc. It is also very useful for covering other items and adds a soft feel to solid objects and hard surfaces.
Covering wooden boxes is easy. First print onto the fabric you wish to use (you could add embroidery to this too!). Remember, fine weave absorbent fabrics will reflect the most accurate printed image. If any part of the print needs strengthening use the wax blocks like crayons to add colour and then fix by ironing over with tissue between the fabric and iron. The stylus tip works directly on the fabric drawing strong solid lines or applying areas of dense colour.

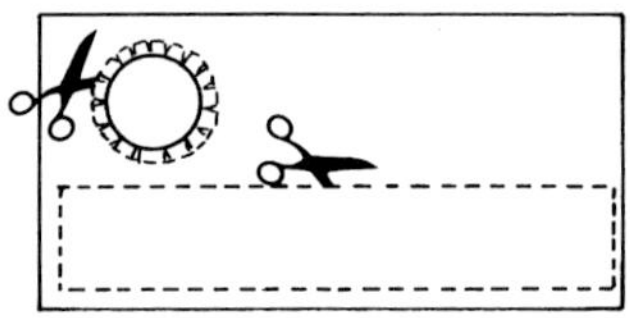

You will need:
- I box and lid for covering
- enough material to cover the box and wrap around the outside
- 3 lengths of matching ribbon or banding each long enough to wrap around the box
- scissors, pencil and glue

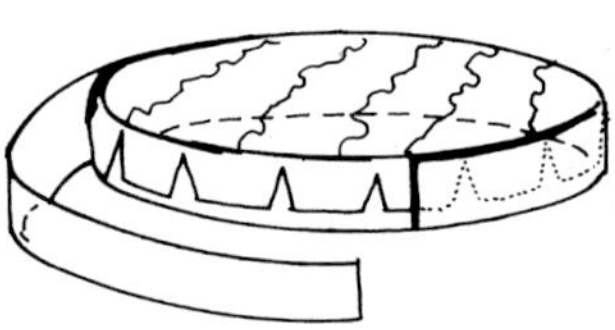

Measure around the box then cut your material slightly larger then needed. Do the same for the lid allowing an extra 1/4" or 6mm all round.
Print this fabric with some strong coloured but harmonius abstract designs (more specific images could be used if desired).

Place the lid centrally on the underside of the fabric and draw around in pencil. Cut small 'V' shapes from the outside almost to the line. Stick the fabric onto the lid also gluing the flaps down on the edge. Wrap the ribbon around the edge, cut to fit perfectly and stick in place.

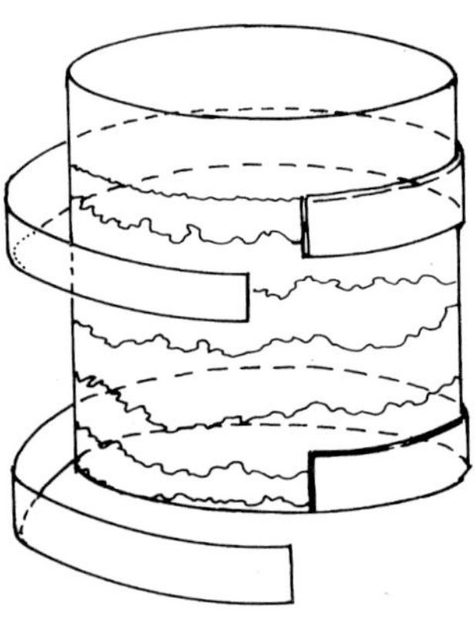

Put the covered lid on the box. Measure from the bottom of the lid to the bottom of the box. Cut the covering fabric in a strip 1/4" or 6mm narrower. Stick this strip centrally around the box. Then trim and stick the end piece overlapping the fabric by about 1/2" or 12mm. Measure, cut and stick matching ribbons or band at the base of the box and directly under the fitted lid. (the base could also be covered).

PAINTING DIRECTLY ON A WOODEN BOX

Wood was the support material used by the Ancients for their encaustic portraits. Modern products of plywood and fibre boards have created extremely stable supports suitable for encaustic art. Encaustic Art waxes can be applied directly onto wood which will provide a good "key" for the medium. If the surface is extremely absorbent it is best to prime and seal it with a coat of white acrylic or a mix of 30% white wood glue and 70% water.
Wooden boxes are readily available in many craft/hobby outlets and provide interesting opportunities for decoration and embellishment. It is not generally necessary to prepare the surface of these items. Varnish provides an attractive finish for the areas not being painted and makes removal of unwanted wax much easier.
The iron, stylus, hot air gun and cold brushes can all be used on wooden items. For this first exploration of working encaustic on wood use the iron and stylus with brush head. The wax needs to be applied quite thickly to avoid seeing through to the natural grain underneath.

Remove the lid of the box and if you wish to protect the edges from getting waxed stick a strip of masking tape (adhesive paper tape) to cover the edge.

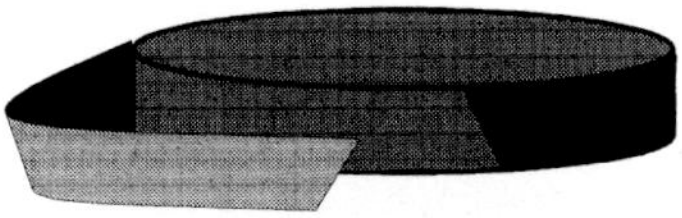

Start with a simple landscape to get the feel of working on a rigid surface. First the sky - using plenty of white wax with a little colour. Then apply the land section. You will find that dabbing for foreground effects is much harder, because unlike the card base the rigid wood can not 'peel' off the iron - instead it 'snaps' off, leaving a pattern of small dots.

When the image is finished remove the tape from the edge and brush on colour all around with the heated brush head. Decorate with further details if desired and finish by lightly polishing. If the box is likely to be knocked or scratched protect the artwork with a sprayfix or varnish the wax. Next try some abstract designs and experiment with some stylus tip details.

A—Z.....

COATING EGGS, BALLS & SOLID ITEMS

Several methods can be used to decorate and paint solid forms like eggs and balls or any other smooth shaped items. These decorated objects may be hung for Seasonal decorations or arranged as interesting collections in a more sculptural manner.
Use egg or ball shapes for the initial trails. As well as natural egg shells many other materials are available in these shapes. Polystyrene and hard plastic (hot air may melt!), wood, ceramics, metal, etc.

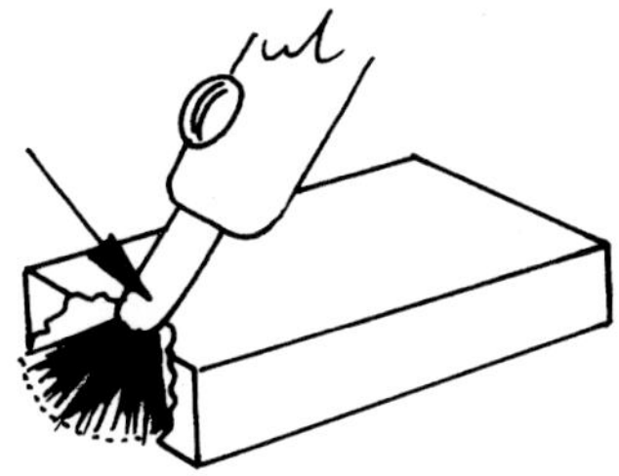

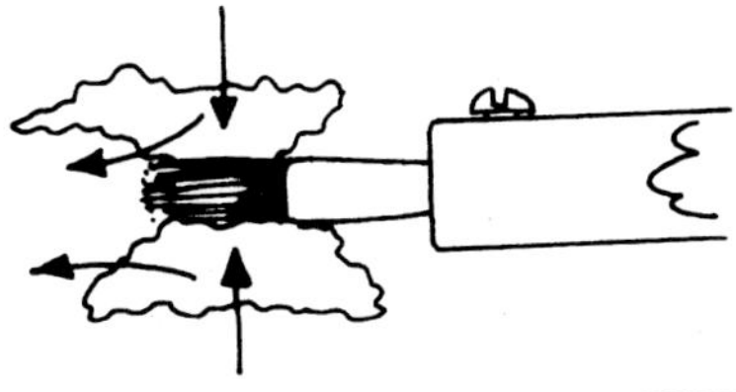

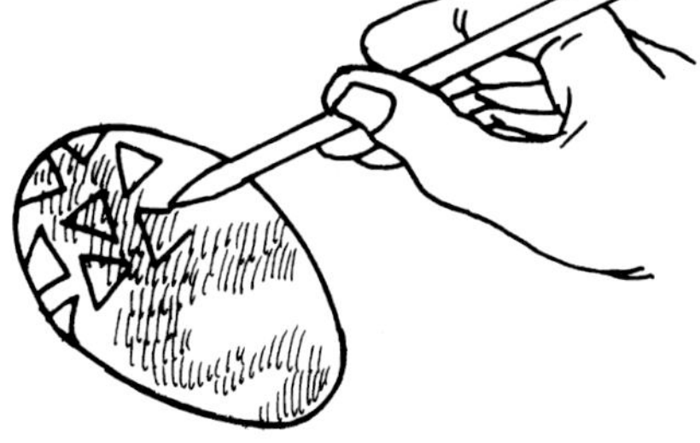

Use the heated brush head in the stylus to apply a very thin coating of coloured wax onto an egg. Use white first then blend in two more compatible colours. This is an excellent opportunity to explore colour mixing (see page 59 for basic colour mix combinations). Remember: work slowly and softly with the brush head. If the object is solid, warm it slightly before starting. To fill the brush with colour more quickly and to avoid 'tangling' the copper fibres place the solid heel of the brush head onto the wax block. To clean the brush head melt on plenty of clear wax and gently wipe the fibres in a tissue pad, always stroking them in a straight direction away from the tool.

Another approach is to first colour the egg with permanent ink marker colours.
Then apply a very thin coat of wax (to avoid flaking off).
Finally use a scribing tool to scratch designs through the wax revealing the colours underneath.

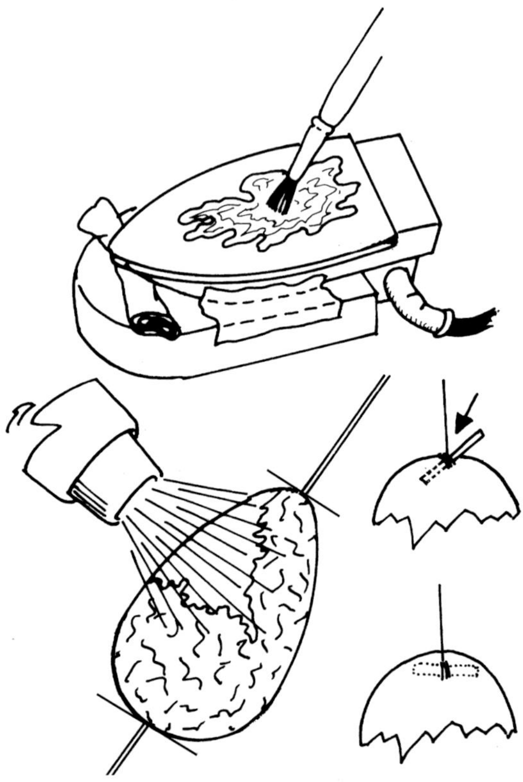

Encaustic art brushes (natural hair) can also be used to paint objects.
Detatch the iron's handle, lay the handle flat on your table. Turn the iron upside down and slide the baseplate into the handle so it sits like a small hotplate. Secure in position with adhesive tape along the edge and make it level by placing tissue under the tip as needed.

Place a spike through a small hole in one end of an egg or ball. A 4" (100 mm) wood screw provides an excellent tool for holding eggs or other solid items. First make a small hole in the object then gently screw until it feels firm and holds the item securely. This method provides a safe 'handle'.
Coat with wax using the iron as a 'palette'. Melt waxes directly onto the upturned base and quickly brush onto your object. Once covered blow hot air using a hot air gun or paint stripper. This should be done very gently to allow the waxes to blend (some may drip off onto the table!). Protect with a sprayfix or varnish if desired.
Remove the spike/screw and glue in a thread 'tie' for hanging.

BLOWING HOT AIR FLOWERS

It is exciting to explore the use of other heated tools. Hot air is available from hair dryers, paint strippers, fan heaters, etc. Hot air melts the wax without touching the card so leaves no tool marks. The temperature, volume of air and shape of the air flow all affect the manner of working. The smaller the nozzle the more concentrated the air flow. Many complex techniques are possible but in this experiment a professional quality hair dryer will normally work quite well.

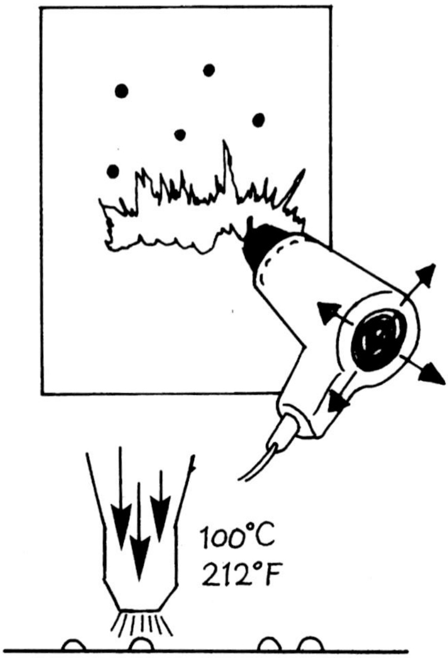

Apply about 8 or 10 small drops of coloured wax to the card with the tip of the iron (3 to 4 mm - 1/8" dia.). Try red and yellow.
Turn on the hair dryer at a hot setting (100C/212F) or a hot air gun at a cool setting. If you have a round reducing nozzle have this fitted.
Hold the nozzle directly over a wax drop and watch carefully as it starts to melt. Move the nozzle around very slightly in an attempt to control the direction in which the wax moves. Try to encourage the wax form from each drop to move in the same general direction. These are the flower heads. When you have completed blowing all the dots an abstract or 'splash' effects should exist.

The may look rather indistinct. The trick is to use the stylus to insirt some 'stamen'. These small dark lines are in the centre's of flowerheads. Even a complete mess of colour can be given form with this technique. Look carefully at the painting on page 45 to see how the 'stamens' give a 3D quality to these otherwise abstract effects.

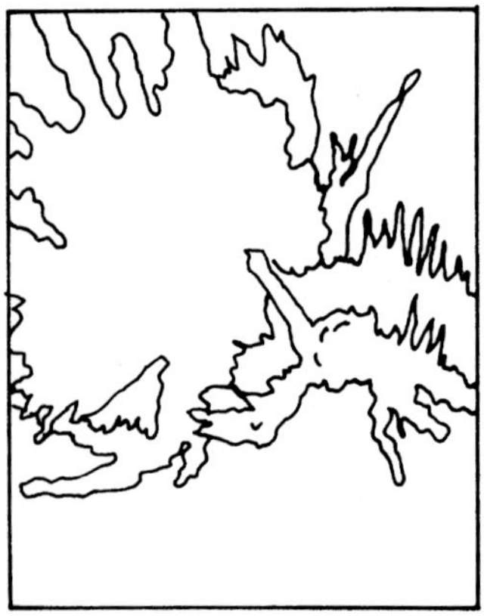

Finally add leaves by sliding the iron's edge through green wax and applying lines until you feel the foliage is finished.

HOT AIR BLOWN SKY

Hot air techniques are excellent for creating large areas of smooth flowing colour. These qualities are important for larger skies and provide fantastic backgrounds for fantasy works. However these blown and dribbled wax effects can remain abstract if you prefer that style.
It is vital to use clear wax as a liquefier. The basic method is to cover the required card area with a good coating of clear wax medium. Then melt and dribble coloured waxes on top of this coating. Place the card onto a rigid board for stability and blow with hot air. Use of higher temperatures creates a very liquid wax which can be "panned" around to create dribbled effects.

Cover the sky area with a good coating of clear wax medium. Then use the iron to dribble on coloured wax in the rough areas requiered. For skies ensure there is plenty of white or light coloured wax at the 'bottom' of the sky area. When completed place your waxed card onto a rigid board (perhaps thick card board) covered with disposable paper.

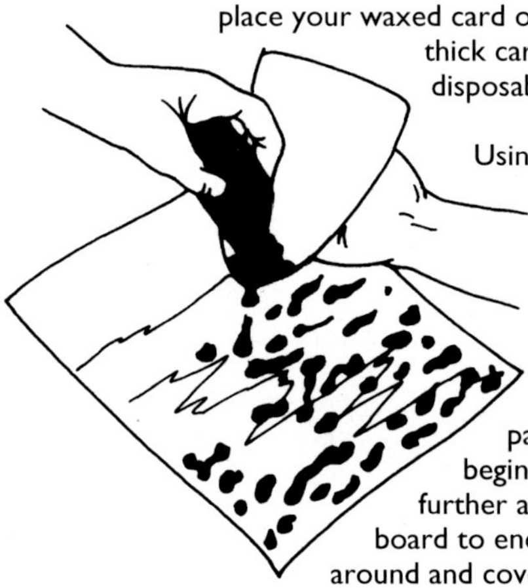

Using the hot air gun (or a paint stripper) carefully blow the hot air at the wax (see page 49). Work in a well ventilated area. Do not direct the hot air at only one spot but instead keep the airstream 'dancing' (see page 49). As soon as the wax begins to melt move the heatgun further away and tilt the rigid under board to encourage the wax to flow around and cover the card required. Work above a piece of disposable paper placed upon your work table - then if any wax dribbles off the card it will not matter. The more steeply you tilt the board the quicker the wax will flow.

For good light in the sky finish by blowing and dribbling the white or lighter wax from the 'bottom' up into and over the darker sky colours. If the sky is too 'busy' it will look unreal so try to keep the wax flow in one general direction.

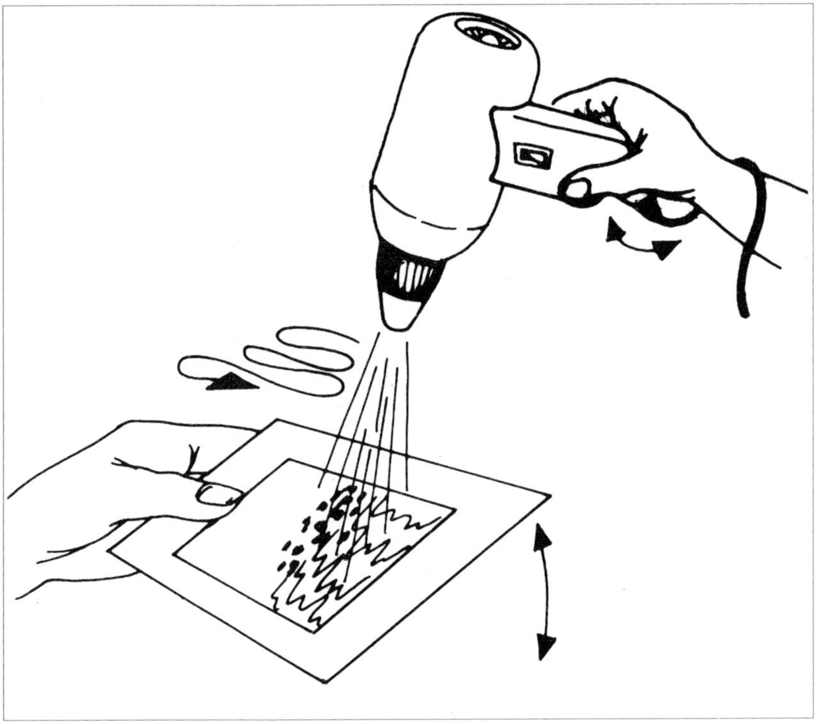

For fantasy backgrounds simply cover the whole card with clear wax and then wax colours. Work with the hot air until they all merge in a pleasing manner. If the wax smokes it is too hot!

Either leave as an abstract design or work into the background with details that suit the colours and respond sympathetically to the 'feel' of the background effect.

Hot air guns can be dangerous – the nozzle can become hot enough to give a very nasty burn, so place the gun well away from yourself and others, whilst it cools. Always work in a well ventilated room.

WORK ON ALTERNATIVE SURFACES

Coloured gloss card – So far all the examples on card have been made using Encaustic Art white card. When other colours are used the images become backlit and highlighted in the chosen colour. Many art shops sell high gloss coloured cards. These tend to be completely non-absorbent and may not provide sufficient "key" for long term artwork so experiment and be aware of this possible problem (the wax may eventually flake off).
However for short term works these cards will provide some lively alternatives and look very different. Remember, the card colour will affect the apparent colour of the waxes. Green wax on a red card will appear almost black. Yellow wax on a blue card will look green and red wax on a yellow card can appear orange.

Clear plastic sheet – Plastics are heat sensitive so care must be taken in choosing the correct materials. Use the iron at the lowest workable heat and complete the work with quick strokes so that the heat is not in contact with the plastic long enough to buckle or melt it.
You can paint backwards on clear plastic. Work the waxes on one side but view the image from the other. This method also offers good protection from scratching. Panels can be made for hanging on the window but do remember that the wax will still melt if the sunlight causes a temperature above 62°c / 140°f. Spraying with a fixative can help prevent damage in this situation.

Absorbent paper – Although Encaustic Art card is non-absorbent other absorbent types of surface may be used to achieve different styles and effects. Remember that when absorbent surfaces are used no changes are possible since the wax has penetrated the fibres of the material and become "ingrained".
Try working on watercolour paper. Wax is a resist to water so if a watercolour wash is applied over the wax interesting effects and images can result.

Other surfaces – Wood and fabric have already been introduced but metal, glass, coloured plastics, man made composition boards of plaster or wood, even stone. All offer different potentials.

ENCAUSTIC WITH RUBBER STAMPS

Rubber stamps enable anyone to produce a good graphic detail without the need to draw. Simply choose a stamp, ink the rubber face and gently but firmly press the stamp onto your card to print the image. In about a minute it is dry and ready for development with encaustic techniques. Waxes can be ironed and crayoned over the stamps without affecting them. Mix clear wax medium with the colours for an excellent translucent result. Some pigments like white are opaque so will obscure the stamped image. When this occurs use the scribing tool to remove the wax and reveal the undamaged stamp underneath.
Try the following ideas. Your stamps may differ so adapt the images to suit your own collection. Gloss coloured cards provide interesting backgrounds for this technique too!

Print an image of a tree slightly off-centre and little below the middle point. Apply sky with the rubbing technique (page 54). Use dark blue wax and work down to the bottom of the tree. Iron on a simple landscape to meet the base of the stamped tree image. Dab in a foreground and add a few grasses and birds if you wish.
Use the scribing tool to scrape off any wax on the tree trunk. Crayon in this part with brown wax. Use yellow and green blocks to crayon over the leaf area of the tree.

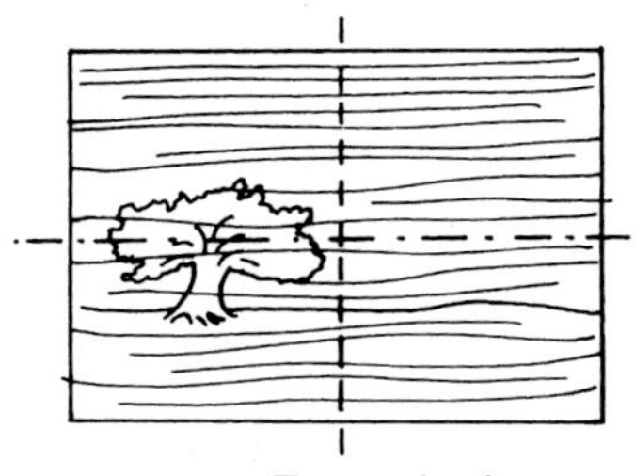
Tree in landscape

Print a cat slightly below centre of your card. Use clear wax medium on the iron and add a little colour - try red and yellow for a sunset. Apply the waxed sunset over the upper card and stamped image. Now dab stronger colours like orange, green, red and brown to cover the bottom of the cat and fill in to the base of the card. Scrape of the wax that covers the cat by use of the scribing tool. Add some grasses from the side of the card by sliding the iron's edge through green wax first. Crayon some yellow or orange wax on top of the foreground detail to reflect the sunset colour (Colour examples on page 55. – Dragonfly detail on page 53).

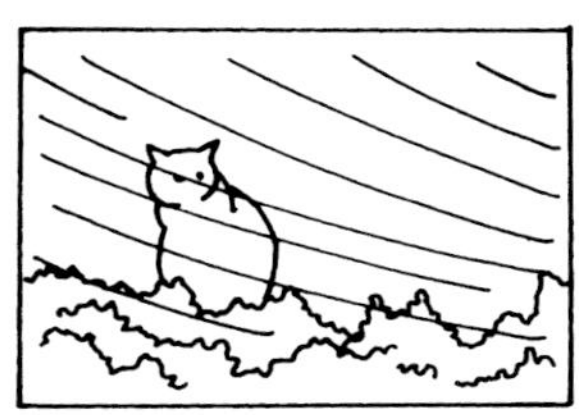
Cat at sunset

RUBBER STAMPING CONTINUED

Underwater scenes are easy to paint and offer an interesting setting for a whole variety of forms. Coloured dabbing effects for coral, wavy grass effects for seaweed, etc.

Underwater whale - stamp or draw some whales (or other underwater creatures) in the centre of the card. Apply a generous amount of clear wax to the iron and mix in a little dark blue and blue green. Smooth this over the whole card in one go, working in one direction. Continue stroking the coloured wax until the texture resembles underwater.

Melt some new blue green and dark blue wax onto the iron and dab a border around the card. This coral or cave mouth effect provides a convincing frame for these images of underwater life.

Rubber stamps and black or coloured silhouettes provide focused centrepiece for seasonal cards. A Christmas image could be camels with wise men, shepherds, or perhaps a nativity scene.

Nativity scene - print or draw a nativity scene just below middle centre of your card. Apply clear wax to iron. Allow a portion as wide as the scene to remain clear.
Work either side adding narrow bands of yellow and finally fill in the remaining bands with dark blue.
Smooth this colour gently in one direction over the card to form a 'heavenlay beam of light' falling on the scene.
Underneath the nativity image dab some foreground using colours that harmonise with the yellow and blue.
Try experimenting with this 'banding' technique using other colour combinations.

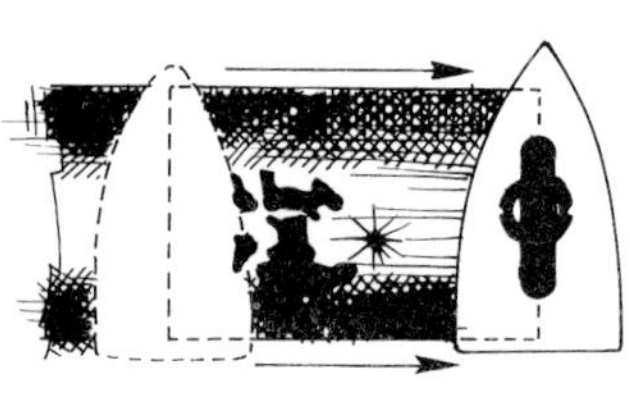

BORDERS WITH STAMPS, EMBOSSING, ETC.

The presentation of your Encaustic Artwork can greatly influence the feel of the image. Adding decoration to the surround whether for a card or a framed painting will change the way it is enjoyed by the viewer.
Embossing is an attractive way to add features to the surround. Ornamental scrolls and corners greatly enhance the presentation. Rubber stamps can be embossed by use of special powders that stick to the stamp image and puff up when heated. Coloured liquids in tubes are available for applying designs to fabric and card. Just trace or draw a design onto the border, apply the coloured applique liquids and activate the embossed effect with heat. Embossing tools can be used to press and work designs into the actual surface of the card. These products are all readily available in craft/hobby shops. Look around for ideas on cards, photos, books and magazines or framed paintings but start with these simple border corners and details.

Images can be associated with the encaustic artwork within the card or framing mat. They can be stamped, drawn, painted or cutout and stuck to the border area. For a simple seascape you could use associated images of dolphins, seahorses, boats, birds, etc. For landscape try flowers, trees, animals, figures or anything which communicates your idea more clearly. Calligraphy writing for greetings or stars, bells and ribbons for Christmas,etc.

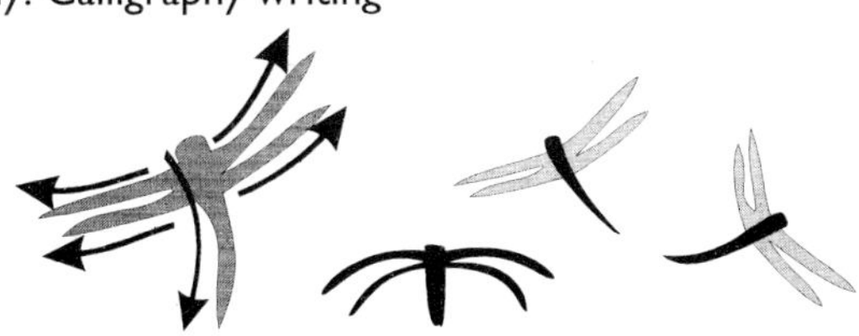

Another striking technique is to spill the painting out onto the border. The small dragonflies offer a useful motif for this idea, but grasses, flowers and birds all make the final result more attractive. For dragonflies use gold or silver wax in the stylus drawing tip. Place a small dot on your card. Then "flick" two close lines to the right and two more opposite lines to the left. Finally take another colour and add a curved body, again using a flick stroke. Do not make downward curved wings or thick vertical body shapes – these will look more like parachuting spiders!

BLACK PEN SILHOUETTES

Silhouettes are simple to draw because they are merely outlines filled with a dark colour. Any image can be traced and coloured black to provide your silhouette, even a photograph.

Use permanent markers, ink pens or fibre tips. Draw your silhouette onto the card, allow it to dry then paint the encaustic image over it. Remember, use clear wax added to colours to create lighter more translucent colourings. Use stronger and darker colour to blend the bottom part of the silhouette into the image. Opaque colours (anything mixed with white for instance) will obscure the image and may need to be scraped off the silhouette afterwards.

RUBBING TECHNIQUES

Encaustic art waxes are extremely versatile. This exercise uses the waxes cold like crayon. Use dark blue and red violet to create a soft sky effect. The darker colours contain very strong pigments and are easiest to use.

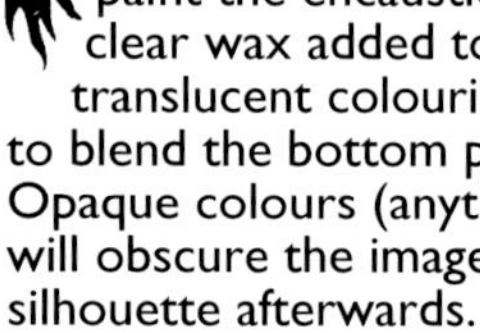

Clean and soften the wax by rubbing one corner/edge hard on a piece of paper (as shown here). Gently crayon the wax to form a soft indistinct colouring with no hard lines. Try the top 25% band in blue, then overlap 1/2 of this with red violet and continue with this new colour to complete another band.

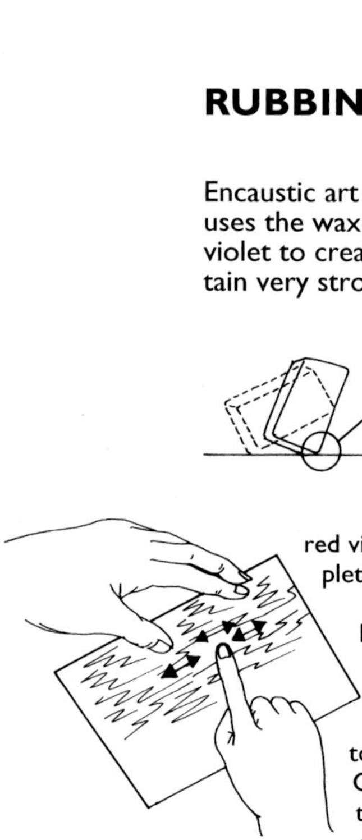

Now smudge these colours together in horizontal strokes, rubbing hard with your finger until all the colours blend. Hold the card down with your other hand either side of your working area to avoid buckling the card.

Complete the image with landscape or use this technique to apply soft backgrounds all over your card.

Arts Encaustic International
5683 PN, Best, The Netherlands

RUB AWAY LAKE

Rubbing the wax whilst hot with a tissue can be used in several interesting ways. Ideal for skies, lakes, backgrounds for stylus drawings, abstracts, etc. If you wish to completely remove an area of wax simply apply heat with the iron and use a tissue pad to wipe off the liquid wax. Try this landscape with a simple cold rubbed sky and a hot rubbed lake.

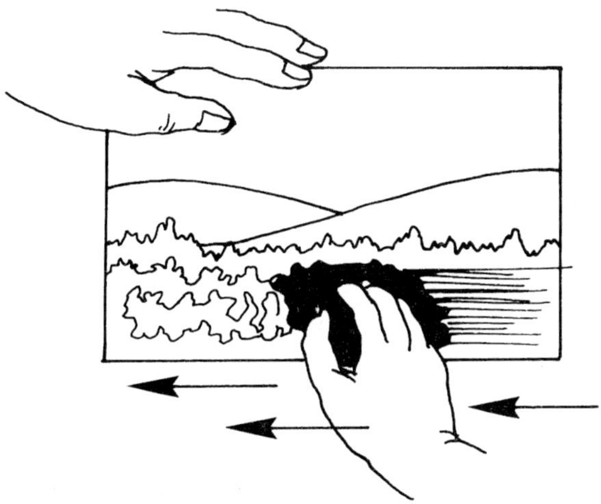

Apply a landscape background of hills at least half way up the card. Next dab in a foreground. These forms are the trees. If necessary use more wax on the iron to ensure they look strong. Now work quickly whilst the foreground wax is still quite hot and soft. Pick up a tissue pad and gently wipe a horizontal line through the lower tree area.

Work lightly and try not to remove all the wax. Then with increasingly stronger wipes work down the card making its surface lighter and lighter. Finally add small detail with dabbed foliage along part of the bottom.

ROCKY MOUNTAIN HORIZON & LAKE

The horizon creates a great deal of character around which the rest of the landscape revolves. A flat landscape, rolling hills or high rocky mountains, etc. The iron can be used to great effect for creation of these different forms. The flat and rolling types are done with the iron sliding but now learn to use the iron's tip and the edge just behind the point.

Load the iron with white, pink and light blue to form a liquid pool as shown.
Hold the iron horizontal.

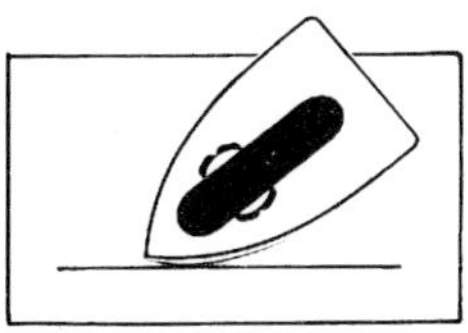

Swiftly place the iron's edge on the leftside of your card (rightside for left handers).

Move the iron sideways in slow jerky irregular movements. Keep the iron tilted high enough to force the wax to flow down onto the working edge. Move slowly and if you run out of wax load the iron tip area with more. Erratic sharpe shapes are good in this context.

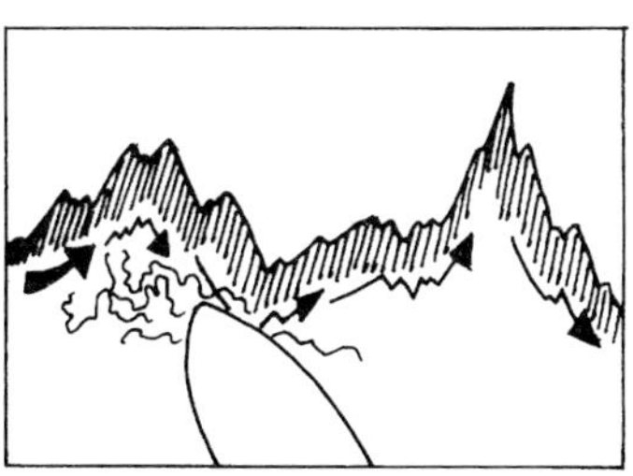

Use the iron's tip to smudge and blend the bottom of the Rocky Mountains down the card and fill in the bare spaces below the horizon.
Use the iron at a much flatter angle.

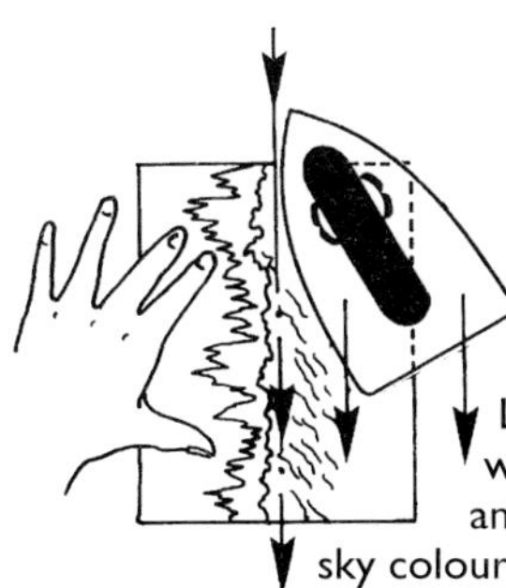

To add a lake turn the card round. Load the iron with white wax and a touch of sky colour. Slowly and with great care smooth the iron across lightly keeping perfectly parallel to the top of the card. For stronger colour repeat using more wax.

FANTASY CASTLES & LANDMARKS

Encaustic Art enables wonderful fantasy images to be created. Abstract effects and techniques can be incorporated into the structure of landscape then clothed with fantasy images (fairies, dragons, castles, etc). The colours used for fantasy do not have to be realistic - so your imagination can run wild and nobody can criticise since it is personal fantasy!

In a more formal but equally fun way famous landmarks or "elements" can be incorporated into images. Use the stylus to copy some of the examples given then find others of your own.

The one vital pattern for success is to blend your object perfectly into the underlying landscape. For instance a dark castle should "grow" out of a dark area in the landscape whereas a light structure or "element" should stem from a light area. As a basic guide remember "dark out of dark, light out of light, dark over light and light over dark". This formula will help your paintings appear stronger and more convincing as illusions.

Create a simple landscape in strong colours. Make the top bands lighter and closer together. As you work down increase their width and strength of colour. Add the castles or 'elements' of your choice, being sure to use a similar colour to blend the bases into the landscape. You can mix colours together on a piece of card with the stylus tip. This wax can be remelted and used any time. Use the stylus to create the fine details required. Keep the castles parallel with the card edges or they will appear to be falling over! Remeber - the foreground elements must be much larger and stronger than their repeats in the distance.

ADDING PERSPECTIVE & DEPTH

As you practise the various styles of landscape covered so far and try your hand at incorporating the rubber stamps, silhouettes and stylus graphics it will become apparent that sometimes something is lacking in the illusion. This is usually due to insufficient or inconsistent information within the image. For instance no distance or shadows. Confusion develops and the image is judged ineffective and unsuccessful.
So look at these basic systems used throughout the world of painting and drawing.

A vanishing point is the spot where all the linesgoverning perspective join (on the horizon in this image). All the lines radiate from that point. The further from the vanishing point the larger each feature grows. This uses just one vanishing point - try it!

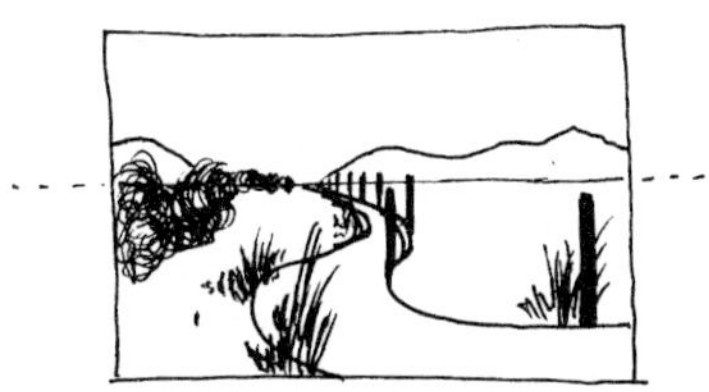

Still using only one vanishing point this image deviates from the simple straight lines and develops the idea using curves. The vertical 'elements' have been used to cut through and over the curves radiating from the vanishing point. Depth is improved whilst the landscape image is softe-ned. Breaking horizontal lines with vertical lines always adds strength and power to the image.

Working from the top downwards try to create contrasting bands of alternating dark and light effect. This improves depth. Remember, tones which measure the strength of dark and light can easily be equal even when colours are different.

3D DETAILS AND SHADING

In everyday terms we describe our environment which is space, as being three dimensional. These three dimensions are height, width and depth. We work on a flat two dimensional surface so somehow the third dimension has to be communicated. This is achieved with perspective and shading.
Shade could be described as the absence of reflected light. So for simplest shading the light must come from one direction. All surfaces toward the light will be pale compared to those surfaces hidden from the light which will be dark. Remember, in a landscape the sky will influence where the light originates from. Use the Stylus and drawing tip to practise on a straight and curved form with this post and tree exercise.

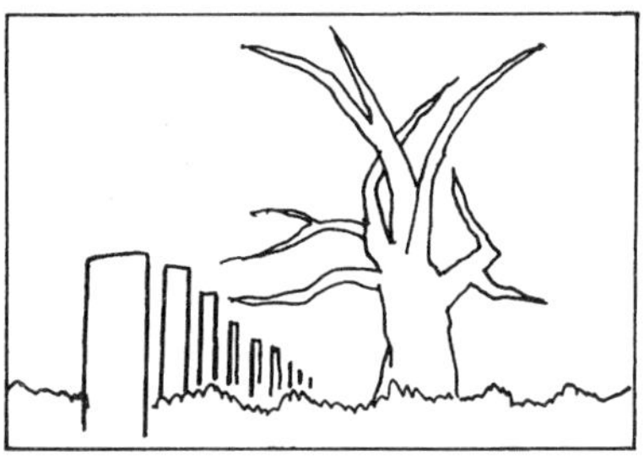

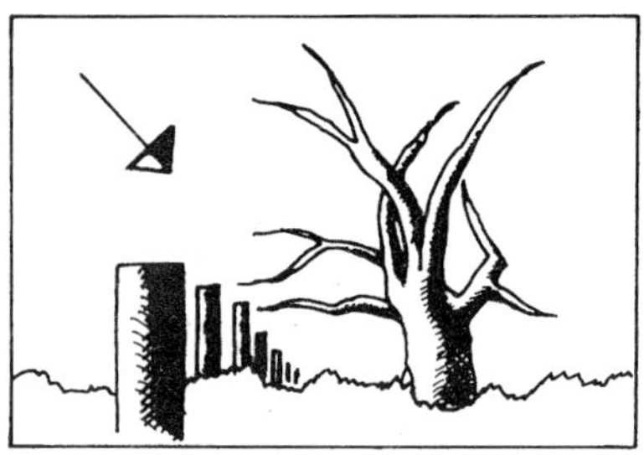

If you have made a sky and landscape the light direction will already be visable. Try this first without a sky - it is simpler. Draw a tree and posts (or some other simple element) using a light brown colour. Refer to books, photographs or even trace it if necessary.

Once the basic image is made use dark brown and black on the stylus tip. Choose a direction for the light as shown by the arrow in this sketch. Darken all sides of your image hidden from the arrow direction. Now use white and highlight all lines facing the arrow. Blend carefully to obtain as even a transition from light to dark as possible.

The image now looks more real and feels less flat, more three dimensional.
Look around you and notice the shadow on buildings or in your house move an object around a light and watch the change.

PLANNING LARGER WORK

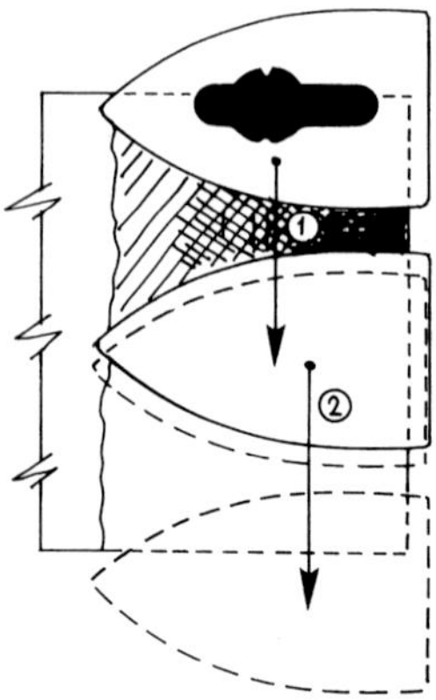

To paint larger Encaustic art images plan an outline approach. Choose the colours you wish to use together and prepare a mental sequence for building up the image. As an example look at how this larger and more detailed landscape was formed. Be brave enough to stretch yourself but try to remain flexible enough to incorporate any "lucky accidents" that occur during working.

On larger paper the iron may not contain enough wax to cover the complete sky area in one go. It is then necessary to load the iron more than once and apply the wax colour in a series of strokes. When the whole area is covered 'float' the iron over the waxes moving slowly and steadily, allowing the colours to blend together where they meet.
Alternatively use the hot air gun technique described on earlier pages to blow the wax colours softly together.

Backgrounds for encaustic paintings are normally created by working from top to bottom over the card. Details are then applied over the background. The sequence for this picture would be:

1 sky with iron or hot air
2 background horizon/hills/mountains
3 lake (made here with the iron)
4 dabbing for trees
5 finer dabbing for middleground foliage
6 rubaway stream using tissue (whilst wax is still warm)
7 vertical stroke to create waterfall effect
8 create an edge to the waterfall. Add foreground foliage
9 develop stream from bottom of waterfall
10 add final foreground with dabbing
11 make grasses with iron's edge
12 details with stylus tip: tree, fence, flowers, dragonflies
13 crayon in light colour highlights on top of background/stream (e.g. pink, yellow)

DEVELOP YOUR SKILL AND ART

Encaustic Art is so versatile that this book has only touched on some of the possibilities. Following projects and ideas is fine but to be truly creative you must also try to develop some of your own ideas. Look around you and start to see with new eyes. The world is full of lines, shapes, colours and patterns. Look at other types of art and craft work. Be experimental, the materials are not expensive and changes can always be made when the non-absorbent card is used.

Enthusiasm is the key to hobby.

Practise is the key to skill.

Awareness is the key to art.

As you develop these qualities remember that self honesty is the key to learning. Ask others for their opinions of your work and be willing to listen to their comments. However, always remember that your unique creative qualities are a reflection of yourself and in the end follow your heart.

If you have any ideas you think others would enjoy sharing send us an example or just write a simple explanation to the Arts Encaustic address in the front of this book.
If you have suggestions or requests for the next book or comments about this one please do write to us. Arts Encaustic Int., Michael Bossom, Glogue, Dyfed SA36 OED, Wales, UK.

Arts Encaustic USA, Gayle Cronin, 7426 Sunset Avenue, Suite C, Fair Oaks, California 95628, U.S.A.
Tel 916-8630411 Fax 916-8635309.

We may not be able to reply personally but your input and help will add to the future of Encaustic Art and its continuing development.

As hobby, as craft, as art, in therapeutic situations and in education many lives are being changed by the passing influence of Encaustic Art.